PARENTING THREADS

CARING FOR CHILDREN WHEN
COUPLES PART

Editors

Erica De'Ath and Dee Slater

Published by

STEPFAMILY
Publications

THE NATIONAL STEPFAMILY
ASSOCIATION

Published by
STEPFAMILY Publications
National Stepfamily Association
72 Willesden Lane, London NW6 7TA, England

Printed by Blackfords of Cornwall Tel: 0726 63638
Designed by Ravenscourt Design London W6
Illustrations by Simon Fell & Paul Christie

ACKNOWLEDGEMENTS

The following people were involved in writing this book:

Pippa Bagnall, Vice Chair, Health Visitors & School Nurses Group, stepchild

Robin Blandford, Family Mediator, Magistrate and stepfather

Imogen Clout, Family Lawyer and stepchild

Christopher Clulow, Director, Tavistock Institute of Marital Studies

Thelma Fisher, Conciliation Co-ordinator, National Family Conciliation Council

Margaret Robinson, Family Therapist, author, and stepmother

Donna Smith, Family Therapist, author, stepmother and grandmother

Eddy Street, Child Clinical Psychologist, divorced , single parent, then remarried

Sarah Tate, Gloucester Probation Service: Court Welfare Service

We are extremely grateful to all members of the Working Group who gave so generously of their expertise and creativity in writing this book in addition to the day to day support and advice they already give to so many parents and couples in families and stepfamilies.

Thank you also to all those members of STEPFAMILY who read early drafts of the manuscript and to those who attended the conference to hear about this book and give their suggestions and comments.

We also gratefully acknowledge support from the Carnegie UK Trust and the Calouste Gulbenkian Trust (UK) in funding this important contribution to helping parents care for their children at a time of change which is often stressful.

STEPFAMILY is the only national organisation providing support, advice and information for all members of stepfamilies and those who work with them. There are local contacts and groups in Northern Ireland, Scotland, Wales and England.

4

STEPFAMILY AIMS TO:

promote a positive image of stepfamily life

support practical step-parenting

encourage research into and information on remarriage and stepfamily life

provide training materials and events for those working with stepfamilies

STEPFAMILY OFFERS A WIDE RANGE OF SERVICES TO MEMBERS:

confidential telephone counselling

2 newsletters:
STEPFAMILY for adults
STEPLADDER for children

local support groups

information packs, books and leaflets

conferences, seminars and training workshops

Membership is open to all who wish to support our aims above.

For further information contact:
STEPFAMILY, 72 Willesden Lane, London NW6 7TA

Telephone:
071 372 0844 (Office) 071 372 0846 (Helpline)

ANNUAL MEMBERSHIP AT 1992:

£15.00 for an individual   £20.00 for couples

£30.00 for Associate Membership
(professional, voluntary or statutory bodies)

CONTENTS

PARENTING THREADS:
CARING FOR CHILDREN WHEN COUPLES PART

Separation and divorce are adult solutions to adult problems. A marriage may have ended but the parental thread linking parent and child is still there.

Differences and conflict are an inevitable part of family life. How adults deal with conflict when they separate has a big impact on them and on the whole family – parents, children, grandparents.

Sometimes the parenting thread is broken. Sometimes it is tied so tight to one parent that the child is frightened of breaking it if they try to reach out to the other who is living elsewhere. Many families tie themselves in knots because everyone is feeling lost, angry, sad, bitter and alone.

Being a parent is very hard work. There are no easy answers or easy ways of doing it. This book provides some guidelines on how to make sure that no-one in the family is hurt too much by all the changes and sadness that can come when couples with children decide to live apart. Keeping the parenting threads intact depends on information, communication and co-operation.

Family life may be changing, but for most of us being a parent is a job for life. Most children start off living with both their parents who are married to each other. But, every year over 150,000 children under 16 years old have to cope with the separation and divorce of their parents, half of them are aged between 3 and 9 years old. Many children whose parents are not married will see them separate, but there are no official records to tell us how many. On an average day in the UK over 500 children and young people will be affected by parents separating and divorcing, sometimes for the second or third time. About 1.5 million children are currently living with just one parent, and around 2.5 million will be growing up with one or more step-parents by the year 2000.

Erica De'Ath *Director*
National Stepfamily Association
October 1992

"STEP THREE" PARENTING

Welcome to this book on parenting. You probably picked it up because you're going through a period of family change, you're determined to do the best for your children, and you're sufficiently experienced to know that parenting is never a straightforward business. We're assuming you are now in the situation either of no longer living with the other natural parent of your children, or that you are bravely taking on the responsibilities of a parent for children who are not yours. Of course, you may well be doing both. Whichever way, this book is for you: you have reached step three.

What about steps one and two? Those chapters have already been written by you. Step one began when you were a child. You know what you expected of your own parents, and the different ways they rose to (and sometimes failed) the challenge. Step two began when you became a parent. We are assuming you and your partner started a family with someone else and brought that parenting experience — the step two stage – into your present living arrangements.

So, what are you likely to learn from this book? We hope it will help you work out what you need to think about as you take this third step as a parent. Whether you are in the process of separating from your partner, of setting up home on your own, or starting over with someone new we think you should find some useful information in the pages that follow that will help you as adults and the children who are part of your life.

However, we must add a warning! Nothing that is written here should be taken as the last word. The organised appearance of the text should not fool you into thinking that parenting is anything other than a complicated, emotional and disorganised business. The handy size of the book is not intended to tempt you to beat yourself, or other parents, or your ex-partner over the head with it! WE have had enough disagreements in writing it to know that there is no single parenting thread. But we do offer three keywords which run through the text as guides to success:

- Information
- Communication
- Co-operation

Step three parenting is hard work. Few of us have any training and we learn on the job, but there is never a better time to learn than when you are doing it. With so many parents separating and then coming together to form new relationships we need to take stock of what seems to work best for all the children and adults involved.

WHAT IS A PARENT?

Since not everyone reading this book may be a parent let's look first at what the job entails. To do any job well you need to know what is expected of you, a suitable place to start, the skills to get on with it, and an understanding of why the job is important.

Does this sound familiar to you?

WANTED: a responsible person, male or female, to undertake a life-time project. Candidates should be totally committed, willing to work up to 24 hours daily, including weekends. Occasional holidays possible after 5 years service. Knowledge of health care, nutrition, psychology, child development, and the education system essential. Necessary qualities: energy, tolerance, patience and a sense of humour. No training or experience needed. No salary, but very rewarding work for the right person.

Who in their right minds would respond to an advert like that? If that is really what we expect of parents then there are a lot of other things they need to do the job properly. We have summarised just some of them here and you may think of several others.

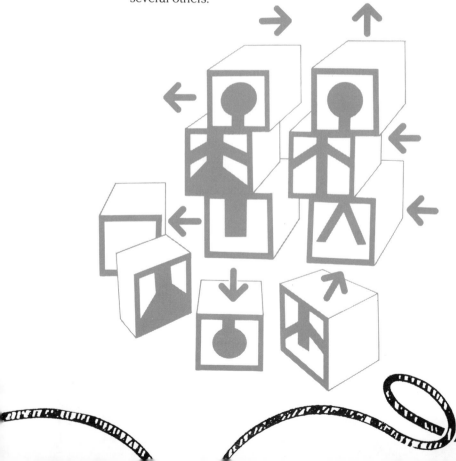

The bare necessities

a warm, comfortable place we call home
a physically safe place for children to grow up
nourishing and healthy food
warm dry clothes
an income to provide these things

Understanding

how our childhood affects the way we behave as adults
how the way we behave as adults affects our children
how to look at what we are doing for the sake of the
   children
how we can make changes easier to manage
how to balance our needs as men and women with what
   children need from parents

Information and knowledge about

looking after children
what children can do at different ages and stages
how to cope with children who are ill, noisy, mischievous,
   naughty
income support and welfare benefits
how to get help from those who are there to provide it –
   doctors, schools, health visitors, playgroups, family
   centres, self-help groups and so on.

Skills

how to give children love and attention
how to listen
how to be firm when necessary
how to talk through problems and difficulties
how to make decisions and accept responsibility for them
how to manage stress, conflict and anger
how to feed a family and pay the bills on a low income
how to balance a job with bringing up children

BEING A PARENT AND PARENTING

Many people have described parenting as the only job we
have for life but it is also a job that changes throughout life and
is different under different circumstances. If you are a parent on
your own, you have all the day to day responsibility and maybe
no-one with whom to share the good times and the bad ones.
When you are trying to share looking after your child or

children with their mother or father (your ex-partner) who is not living with you then that takes some organising. Although you know who is, and is not, their biological parent it may not always be clear who is, and is not, doing the parenting.

The status of parenthood which is absolutely necessary to carrying out the job, depends on the recognition of others. Separation and divorce do not end the duty of each parent to play a full and active role in the upbringing of their children. But the law also makes provision for unmarried fathers, step-parents, grandparents and occasionally others to acquire parental responsibility if they are actually involved in parenting a child.

CHILDREN ACT 1989

PART I, Section 2 Parental responsibility for children

(1) Where a child's father and mother were married to each other at the time of his birth, they shall each have parental responsbility for the child.

(2) Where a child's father and mother were not married to each other at the time of his birth –

(a) the mother shall have parental responsibility for the child;

(b) the father shall not have parental responsbility for the child unless he acquires it in accordance with the provisions of this Act.

(3) References in this Act to a child whose father and mother were, or (as the case may be) were not, married to each other at the time of his birth must be read with section 1 of the Family Law Reform Act 1987 (which extends their meaning).

(4) The rule of law that a father is the natural guardian of his legitimate child is abolished.

(5) More than one person may have parental responsibility for the same child at the same time.

(6) A person who has parental responsibility for a child at any time shall not cease to have that responsibility solely because some other person subsequently acquires parental responsibility for the child.

(7) Where more than one person has parental responsibility for a child, each of them may act alone and without the other (or others) in meeting that responsibility; but nothing in this Part shall be taken to affect the operation of any enactment which requires the consent of more than one person in a matter affecting the child.

(8) The fact that a person has parental responsibility for a child shall not entitle him to act in any way which would be incompatible with any order made with respect to the child under this Act.

(9) A person who has parental responsibility for a child may not surrender or transfer any part of that responsibility to another but may arrange for some or all of it to be met by one or more persons acting on his behalf.

(10) The person with whom any such arrangement is made may himself be a person who already has parental responsibility for the child concerned.

(11) The making of any such arrangement shall not affect any liability of the person making it which may arise from any failure to meet any part of his parental responsibility for the child concerned.

Adults often think of parents as the people who live with their children, get them out of bed in the mornings, comb their hair, cook their meals, wash their clothes, take them to school and so on. When a parent leaves home it can easily seem that he or she has left the children as well as the partnership or marriage. And very often the remaining parent may wish that were so.

The really important people we must remember are, of course, the children.

13

- Who do they think are the most important adults in their lives?
- Who do they regard as being a parent to them?
- Who are they allowed to admit into this role by other family members?

The only people who can answer these questions are the children themselves. The problem is that they will often be confused about this. In any case children will, quite rightly, not want to carry the burden of responsibility, choice and decisions which properly belong to the adults in their lives.

Contrary to how it usually feels, parents – however we define them – are the most important people in the world for most children. More important than politicians, pundits and pop stars, parents hold the past and future in their hands. As children we look to parents to be always there for us. In old age they may be the only people we can recall clearly. Running like a thread through our lives they connect us with our roots, providing some coherence and continuity through the changing seasons of life. Sometimes in the foreground, increasingly in the background as we get older, parents are always present – even when they are absent. How many of us, even as adults, have wished we could call on our mother or father to make everything turn out alright. Partnerships may come and go, but parents are forever. No wonder we have mixed feelings about them!

HOW CAN WE HELP EACH OTHER AS PARENTS?

You may well ask if it is possible to match up to these high hopes that surround parenthood and survive, let alone to do a good enough job. Are the needs we have as adults the same needs that children have? Surely our needs are changing as the family changes and as the children grow older? How can we try and balance all these things when there are lots of practical arrangements to make as well?

There are an awful lot of us trying to do a good job as parents and to rebuild our lives as adults. We don't know exactly how many people are forming stepfamilies after previous relationships have ended. It is likely to be hundreds of thousands. We do know, from research studies, that two years after divorce over 50% of men have remarried and five years after divorce 50% of women. We also know that a great many people choose not to remarry but still want to build a new family life together. So it seems a lot of adults and children are developing new strands of family life as they move from a two parent home, spend some time in a lone parent home, and then move into a stepfamily home.

In this book we will focus on the needs of adults and children particularly as they relate to the often difficult business of reconstructing family life. Perhaps the most important thing to think about is what you can do to help create an emotionally secure environment:

where people can talk about what concerns them
where information can be exchanged
where communication is supportive not destructive
where understanding is developed
where the skills of parenting are firmly rooted in trust and
    respect for each other.

This is a difficult job to do and we've got some suggestions to help you get started and hold on to all the threads.

◑ OLD THREADS: Accepting time past in the present

During periods of personal change and family re-organisation there are three mistakes that can easily be made.

The first is to dwell on the past so that everything that happens in the present, and planning for the future, is dictated by the feelings and images associated with a previous period of personal history. When that period is very recent it is impossible not to be preoccupied by it. Indeed, *it is important to make time to know how you are feeling.* In order to move on, room must be made to rework events and experiences which have been difficult. In particular, if you are to work together just as parents and not as partners then that partnership must be given up and a new co-operative relationship developed, as you continue your role as parents of your children. Problems can arise when old scores continue to be settled by adults through present-day relationships with their children.

The second mistake is to discount the past altogether. The wish to eradicate a past marriage is understandable, particularly

when forming a new partnership. Children often think this means that a relationship with their absent parent is no longer allowed and may protest strongly or stay silent. Clearly one response brings open conflict, and the other a retreat into a private world from which others are excluded. The wish to make everything new, to start all over again, is very powerful for people who are forming new partnerships. *Yet the firmest foundations are built on the security everyone gains from the knowledge that the past can be talked about and is a legitimate and important part of family history.*

15

A third mistake can follow from the previous two. So often people form partnerships and remarry as if it was their very first marriage or partnership. This can deny some of the roots from which the new family has sprung and the different material and relationship environment in which it has to develop. The situation is most strikingly different when there are children. *Family history and family trees are important because they tell us where we have come from, the point of growth that we have reached, and with whom we are connected.*

◐ FAMILIAR THREADS: Consistency

The more parents can work together, the fewer the areas of uncertainty. For children security comes from you being consistent in the way you love and discipline them and being available for them even if from separate homes. This can make even dramatic change manageable for them.

Forming family relationships can involve a lot of uncertainty and anxiety. It is hard to relax about family matters when worrying about money, or work, or housing - all major and potential areas of insecurity for both you and the children. When a question mark is raised about your future as a family or as a parent feelings can become quite uncontrollable, spilling out into other arrangements for the future and adding to the overall sense of insecurity for you and everyone else.

Adults, like children, need their attachments. The more unsettled you feel, the stronger your need is to become securely attached. The bond between you, as a parent, and your children is an especially important type of attachment. If it is threatened, not only is there the risk of losing the children you love but also there is the threat to that part of yourself you and others regard as 'parent'.

Uncertainty about being a parent constitutes a crisis of identity for adults as well as for children. This can create its own problems. Not only is the scope for conflict between you and your ex-partner or current partner increased if the parenting knot is loosened, but the children will also suffer. The more

threatened the attachment the more likely each of you as parent will either cling to or disengage from your children. This can mean that children who desperately need your time, love and concern while going through this stressful change in their family actually get less time from each of you. Either you feel unable to pay attention to their needs or you may stifle their relationship with their other parent by clinging to them too tightly.

◐ NEW THREADS:
Time to learn on the job

One of the myths we grow up with is that parents are born rather than made, that they automatically know what to do so no-one needs to learn what's involved. The consequence is we expect too much, we are very often critical of ourselves and others, and forget that everyone learns on the job. The most valuable learning experience is talking to and receiving help and support from others who have already been through similar stages in life or are going through it right now, like you.

When parents live in different places the ordinary problems of parenting become more complex. This is new ground, and those working it are pioneers in the field. For example, no-one has given much thought to:

- **How parents not living with their children develop and sustain their relationship.**
- **How frequent visits should be?**
- **Where visits should take place?**
- **What advantages and disadvantages are there for children who stay the same amount of time in different homes?**

Both mothers and fathers will have to learn new practical skills if they are to cope on their own.

Everyone needs to be sensitive to the changing needs and commitments of children and parents over time. There is the emotional anguish that can arise at the beginning and ending of contact visits with the repeated experience of separation. We all need to realise and recognise that these things do happen. We need to consult amongst each other if we can to *try to understand each person's needs even if everyone cannot have their own way.* Ironically, the challenge of this new situation means that some parents have strengthened and improved their relationship with their children, while for others it has proved too much emotionally for them to maintain the ties.

For a partner who is taking on parental responsbilities for other people's children there are different kinds of questions:

- **What authority can a parent have over a partner's children?**
- **How can men and women care for children who are not theirs without appearing to usurp the place of the birth parents?**
- **What part can be played in negotiations between the children and their birth parents?**

For some of you these questions may result in tensions which your new partnership may find difficult to manage. Others may discover that you occupy a unique position from which to help and advise on the continuing process of developing family life. You may become a bridge between the old and new family, or just an important extra adult for the children to turn to as they grow up.

Perhaps we need a job description for a step-parent to counter balance the one for a parent.

WANTED: Someone for full-time or part-time position. In either case, a full-time commitment to a parent and their child(ren) is required. Possible to include applicant's own children. Necessary skills: devotion to other people's children; patience; knowledge of adult and child psychology; ability to demonstrate concern for children who may not reciprocate; optimisim, endurance and faith in the future. NB: This position should not be confused with foster or residential care. No previous experience is required. No salary, although a small remuneration is sometimes available through a complicated legal system and is not paid directly to the job holder. Time off can be arranged and is recommended.

◑ DELICATE THREADS: Protected time

It is easy to underestimate the physical and emotional exhaustion that goes hand in hand with step-parenting. The business of remaking family life can involve changes of address, new working patterns, different schools, unfamiliar neighbourhoods, money worries and legal squabbles. All of these on top of an emotionally upsetting experience that many feel is like the whole of life being put through the shredder.

It is hardly surprising that in these circumstances parents sometimes need to be able to shut the door against their children without feeling guilty about doing so. *New partnerships need protected time to feel secure and to flourish.* It is only possible for people to attend to others when they have been adequately looked after themselves and this

should not be a cause for guilt or blame. There will always be some tension between meeting your needs and those of your children. The important thing is to find a balance.

Any period of change involves a remaking of oneself. If the change has been traumatic, self-esteem and self-confidence will almost certainly have taken a bad knock. What we all need at such times is affirmation and reassurance from others. This restores our belief in ourselves and a sense of being valued and valuable. Friends, family and work colleagues may become particularly important in this process. New partnerships may be seen as the solution to personal loneliness and unhappiness. But most people also realise the risks of recommitting themselves before recovering enough of themselves to enter into a new relationship.

By now it will be clear that we feel that children's needs are paramount. We also know it is not always easy to reflect this in day to day caring when going through a period of stress, change and crisis when you, too, need looking after. The next chapters look at what the children need and how together you can go about meeting them as parents who continue to be part of their life: past, present and future. The continuing thread of parenting which is so important to children needs to be unravelled, rewound and respun to create a new family tapestry.

CHILDREN'S NEEDS?

Whatever you are doing between yourselves as a couple, children in your family need to know they are seen as individuals in their own right. Probably the most important message for you is that your children need to know that some things will inevitably change. They need to know some things may change and they need to know that some things will remain the same. At the centre of the sameness is the love of the people who care for them, especially their parents,

When your children have this continuity of parental love and concern they will be better able to accept that family life is going to be different and can more easily adapt to change. This thread of continuity that children need alters as they develop and grow. Very young children need a parent sitting in the room while they find out what's in the corner. Older children need a parent at home while they go shopping on their own. Teenagers need the security of knowing they are loved before exploring personal relationships outside the family.

The threads that bind you together need to be slack enough to let your children explore but sufficiently resilient when they want or need to be pulled back to safety. Your children can then feel cared for and free to test the outside world. You can encourage this when new opportunities are offered. In this way family problems can be eased and the world allowed to become an exciting place which challenges your children to extend and develop their abilities to the full.

Flexibility is the keynote. You need to be able to adapt and modify arrangements both in terms of what you want and expect and what is appropriate for your children according to their age, stage of development and whatever is happening in your family at the time. But **children do need the safety and security of knowing that you, their parents, are in charge and care for them and their well-being.** They can only be sure of this if you keep them informed and show them you are trying to balance their needs as children with yours as adults.

SEPARATION AND CHILD DEVELOPMENT

Continuity of parenting does not mean that two parents have to live in the same house. A good foundation for exploring the world is provided by continuing to give your children the message "you are loved and valued in your own right" and by making sure they receive this message in a way that is fitting to their age. The constant repetition of this message helps children deal with the pain and upset of separation and divorce.

It can feel like the end of the world when children burst into tears, fight with you or become just plain difficult. It's easy to become over-worried about such outbursts of feeling. You may feel they are behaving like this because the other parent is at fault, or that your current arrangements are not working out, or that this is a punishment for you for taking a course of action you knew they didn't want. Their behaviour may signal all these things but more importantly it lets you know that your children need to grieve when they feel they have lost something important to them. They need to know that you understand and can withstand such feelings that even they may not fully comprehend.

When children are very upset they often behave badly in one setting, perhaps at home or at school, but not others. However uncomfortable it is to be on the receiving end of a child's emotional outbursts or tantrums they are actually displaying a confidence in your ability to cope, to take care of them and take account of their fears, anger and anxieties. The most difficult thing for you as a parent is that their powerful feelings may echo your own. It can be very hard indeed to take their distress without blaming yourself or someone else. It may even be difficult to listen to what they want to say while you are trying to control your own feelings of anger, sadness and loss. Stick with it. The best thing you can do is to recognise their distress. You and they have both suffered a loss and you can say this to them even if it is hard to understand. This does not mean you have to be walked over. Children still need to be brought up and that means understanding what is appropriate behaviour for their age at the moment and insisting that basic family rules are still kept.

CHILD DEVELOPMENT AND CONTACT WITH BOTH PARENTS

In the same way that children of different ages need different degrees of continuity and safeguards, so the age of a child makes a difference in terms of the nature of their contact with a parent no longer living at home with them.

Children develop through stages during which their needs for contact with parents change, and the ways in which that can be maintained also change. The following chart is a guide for you to plan continuing parenting contact for your children over the forthcoming years.

AGES	DEVELOPMENTAL CHANGES	CONTACT NEEDS
Birth - 18 months	Children need consistent physical care and a stimulating environment. Through this they learn trust and develop the beginning of their own identity.	Children need to remain more or less in the same place and a frequent and predictable pattern is most suitable.
18 months-3years	Children rapidly acquire new skills as they learn to use their bodies and develop language. Through this they learn a self confident way of dealing with the world.	Consistency and frequency of contact are still very important.
3 yrs-6yrs	At this stage children build on their confidence through a continued development of intellectual abilities. They learn to mix more with children and adults other than parents. They also become aware of a sexual identity.	Children in this age group benefit from highly predictable contact including telephone calls and cards.
6yrs-10yrs	The ability to think about themselves and the world continues, children develop a conscious notion of "who I am". Ethical choices, peer pressures and self discipline are all issues of this period. The child now has a clear idea of being away and separate from parents.	Weekend visits work very well for this group. As above, highly predictable contact including telephone calls and cards can be important.
10yrs-13yrs	As the child approaches puberty, there can be fluctuations of emotions as physical changes occur. Sexual awareness and curiosity as well as the continuing tasks of intellectual and physical growth are all major issues.	Gender differences emerge which may affect contact with the other parent.
14+ years	This phase is often marked by difficult parent/child relationships as the child rebels against parental authority. Adolescents are working very hard at being their own person in their own right.	Flexibility is the name of the game; adolescents who maintain good contact with parents often have variable patterns of visiting and staying.

Please remember:
- these boxes won't tell you about each child's individual temperament, (only you as their parent can know that) but they do give a rough guide.
- contact isn't just about visits or staying over.
- don't expect too much from younger children and be flexible with adolescents
- go for quality.

GUIDELINES NOT RULES: But these are not rules – O.K!

What is clear from all the research on children of separated parents is that *it is not necessarily what you do that counts but how you do it.* Doing it well, having a good relationship with your children and a workable arrangement for yourselves makes all the difference. Some of you may be able to have routine shared care of your children even when they are very small especially if you live very near by. For others, the difficulties of small or cramped accommodation or long distances might mean that younger children rarely get to spend time with the parent not living with them. Time away from home can be distressing for any young child who is not used to being separated from the person who usually looks after them. In such cases it is hard not to take their distress personally. That's why contact of all kinds is important to keep the parenting thread alive through messages, pictures, photos, a voice on the phone so that when a meeting can be arranged it is not a total surprise to your child.

WHAT DOES DOING IT WELL MEAN IN PRACTICE?

If your ex-partner moves away and can't see your children as often as the children would like it is still possible to make sure a good relationship is maintained. It is also much better to only make promises that you know you can keep. Broken promises help nobody and children always deal better with the truth. Many children count the days from one visit or phone call to the next, and are bitterly disappointed and angry when nothing happens as agreed or promised. If you can't do what you've promised then let your children know, don't leave them waiting and wondering whether you've forgotten them or just don't care anymore.

It's also important for you not to moan and groan and complain about each other. It only serves to create divided loyalties for your children. Even when you disagree with something that has happened it is possible to play your part as a parent well. In the long run it will pay dividends for your children and for your relationship with them.

DECIDING, THEN TELLING AND THEN LISTENING

Even before you have made a firm decision about separating or living with someone new you may well have been in a muddled or unusual state and your children will be aware that something is up. It does help to acknowledge this even if you are still not absolutely certain in your mind what is happening or going to happen. At least you can be honest and clear with them and tell them the situation from your point of view. The decision about whether or not to separate, or to remarry, is an adult decision and all the practical tasks that follow from it have to be met by adults.

After deciding comes the telling. Children deal much better with situations if they have had a clear explanation of what is happening and what is likely to happen. They need facts, not emotions or opinions. Obviously as children grow up they can deal with more complicated information. You need to consider this especially when there are several children (in the family) of different ages and at different stages of development.

When parents are separating and divorcing, children always need to know exactly what it means for them in terms of:

- where they will live
- how they will continue to see the parent no longer living at home
- how often they will see them

When a new partner is introduced children need to know:

- that both their parents still love and care for them
- what to call the new partner
- whether they will be moving home or not
- whether and how it will affect their relationship with their other parent

After the telling comes the listening. *One of the basic needs of all children, no matter how young or old, is to*

feel they are being listened to. They need to know that their point of view is understood and accepted. Teenagers are capable and entitled to have a say in where they should live and how their care is managed. That does not mean you have to do everything they ask or never do anything to upset them. It means giving them the time and space to express their opinions on what is happening, and letting them know that you understand if they feel angry with both of you.

Whatever it is you are trying to decide – to separate, to get a divorce, to live together, to remarry – children are not helped in their emotional development if they are told that *they* can make these important decisions. **The law encourages consultation with children but it recognises that they do not have the final say.** In valuing your children by listening to their feelings but not requiring them to make a decision you will help them to cope with adult decisions more effectively.

Again, as with other matters during this time of change and disruption, remember, **it is not the words themselves that are important but how you say it** when explaining your decision. How to reach and agree those decisions is the focus of our next chapter on parenting arrangements.

WORKING OUT PARENTING ARRANGEMENTS

WHY WORK THEM OUT?

When couples separate the sharing of parental responsibility needs to be sorted out. You can still take parenthood for granted as each of you continues to hold responsibility after separation or divorce, but you will have to sort out how to share the everyday care of your children and make financial and other arrangements for yourselves and for them.

Most children, as we saw in the last chapter, need routines and continuity even more after the upheaval of a parental separation than they did before. They need to be able to feel at home with both of you wherever you are living.

You need to plan to keep those parenting threads intact. It is really helpful to children if you can work together to sort out the tangles which inevitably arise. Far better than dropping the threads entirely, or letting them break, or get in such a twisted mess that the whole heap becomes full of knots and tangles and is dumped onto the lap of one of you to sort out alone.

WHO WORKS THEM OUT?

Arrangements for children are best made by their parents! They work best when they are worked out *jointly* by both of you to take account of the particular needs of your children. Further, they are likely to work best when those who are needed to make the arrangements work are consulted.

So you need to consider who to involve in the discussion. It starts with you. Can you sit down together and plan? If not, can a mutual friend or a relative (who does not take sides) help you or do you need outside help from a mediator? (see help available in the index).

If either you or your ex-partner has remarried or has a relationship with a new partner, he or she is likely to have some parenting responsibilities on a day-to-day or occasional basis, even if not holding legal parental responsibility. Step-parents therefore could be consulted about the arrangements even if not directly involved in the actual decision making.

You can involve the children too by consulting them and giving them information about the decisions you make. You might consider making provisional decisions and then consulting the children about them. If you do this they will soon tell you if your suggestions do not suit their plans – for example,

if there are clashes with football or swimming or a school or community activity. If there is something or someone included in your plan that they are not happy about, they can then tell you.

The decisions, however, are your joint responsibility.

WHERE AND WHEN WILL YOU WORK THEM OUT?

Try to find a good time and place – comfortable and possibly belonging to neither of you – and give yourselves enough time.

Difficulties over arrangements often arise because of when and where they are discussed. For example, negotiating arrangements on the doorstep when collecting or returning children is not likely to be the best time and place. The children will be moving between you, leaving one and going to the other and you and your ex-partner may find it painful to see them again or to let them go. Such meetings may evoke feelings about your own separation from each other, whether angry or sad. One or both of you is likely to be particularly vulnerable, especially if the separation is fairly recent. You are not likely to be at your best and it is, after all, the *children's* time.

Arranging a good time and place to plan, away from the children, can also provide a time to swap good news about them. If you only communicate with each other when there is a problem, the focus may only be on difficulties. Part of your planning therefore could include a routine meeting to share information about the children's progress, as well as to discuss any problems that may have arisen.

It could also help your children. Research has shown that children who experience conflict between their parents at times of handover and visits often feel they are the cause of the argument. Some may even try to stop the conflict by stating that they do not wish to see one of you.

WHAT DO YOU NEED TO WORK OUT?

The following is a list of some of the things that parents often discuss. Your family can make a list of the characteristic things that make up your unique family life so you will probably want to add to or ignore things listed here:-

Homes – where, with whom, and when your children are going to sleep, eat, keep their things, play, do their homework and share their personal and everyday experiences. Children can come to feel at home in two places and some do spend half their time with one parent and half with the other. But practicalities of time and place usually mean that they spend more weekday time in one place rather than the other.

Time – when and how long your children are going to be with each of you and how both of you are going to share the everyday and special responsibilities, e.g. going to school meetings.

Grandparents, aunts, uncles, cousins – how your children are to keep in touch with their relations. Family history and traditions are important and children need to retain contact with the wider family; they should not have to lose anyone just because you have separated.

New partners – if either of you remarries the children will gain a step-parent. If either of you has a new partner that person will become part of your childrens' everyday world and the part they take needs to be discussed so that any fears or anxieties are identified and common sense prevails.

Money – how the costs of childrens' daily lives can be met so that, even if everyone is worse off financially, children are protected as far as possible from hardship and reductions in their opportunities.

School, nursery, playgroup, church, community or youth groups and activities – how they will get there, who goes to parents' meetings and evenings, who decides about school functions and trips.

Clothes, toys and special possessions, including pets – who buys them, who keeps track of them.

Doctor, dentist, music teacher, swimming lessons, etc. – who they are, where they are, who takes them, pays for them, organises them.

Birthdays and special days – where they are spent, who organises them.

Cancellations and emergencies – what system you will have for not making a drama out of a crisis!

HOW WILL YOU WORK THEM OUT?

Whether you are sitting down to plan on your own together, or with a mutual friend or relative, or with an outside trained mediator, the following tips might help:-

● Pay attention to how you communicate.

Try to share specific instances of what you want or don't want rather than generalise. For example, if there have been difficulties over the children returning late from visits then discuss particular days and times when the children have been late rather than generalise by saying they are always late.

● Look forward not back.

Try to avoid analysing the past and explaining past difficulties unless they are really of specific relevance to future arrangements.

Go to meetings with a clear agenda and specific proposals. Sometimes it helps to write them down beforehand so that you can work things through calmly.

● Talk together first then consult with others involved.

As we said before, others need to be consulted, but it is better to try and establish *your* planning partnership, as parents with the joint responsibility, rather than going with your "side's" proposals. Try to negotiate as parents, not spokespeople.

● Negotiate firmly, clearly and assertively but avoid tricks and tactics.

Trying to score points off each other will create and reinforce barriers and resistance at a time when negotiation and compromise are needed both for you and your children.

● Focus on the children.

Talk about what you want for them and what you can each realistically offer to do. If there are clashes or gaps in what you can provide, then it helps to stop the discussion and ask "What do the children need?", "What do they want from each of us?","What would they like us to arrange for them and what do we think therefore that we could try to arrange?"

● Try to avoid concentrating on what you do *not* want.

This is especially so if it is something beyond your control; for example your children having contact with your ex-partner's new partner, or a different bedtime or type of diet when they are away from your home (unless there are specific health and dietary needs).

Try to come to terms with the fact that you no longer have a say in everything that happens in your child's life.

Children can accommodate and cope with two separated parents and the introduction of one or two step-parents. But it is much easier for them to do this and to accept two differing regimes if you can also accept that a new adult, whether your new partner or your ex-partner's new partner, has a role in the lives of your children. When your children are with your ex-partner, he or she is responsible for them and that means they can take whatever steps they believe to be necessary in the best interests for the safety of the children.

● If the worst comes to the worst.

If matters arise, when the children are not with you, that have to be challenged for the sake of the children, then face that, tell your ex-partner and if you cannot resolve it by talking, either together or with a mediator, then application can be made to the Court for a Specific Issue or Prohibited Steps order. (see legal aspects on page 49).

● Be prepared to work at making things work.

Soon after separation it is not unusual for people to behave in an uncharacteristic way because of anger and distress. This is especially true if separation is fairly recent, and particularly if only one of you wanted it. Most of us do recover and behave more reasonably in time.

While you cannot undo what has happened in the past you can be optimistic about the future. Of course, if either of you has behaved irresponsibly before or since the separation, through deception or violence, then you will probably not expect to be trusted or trusting straight away. It takes time to rebuild trust and regain respect. However, you can make a commitment to try to deal with issues differently in the future.

If for example arrangements have broken down you may need to try out something new for a while. And you may find that using the telephone to sort things out is difficult. Telephone calls can be experienced as an intrusion. Arranged telephone calls by the adults purely for parental matters can help keep matters calm and can be kept quite separate from calls between parent and child.

Some changes in family lives can be very upsetting for children and therefore are reflected in their behaviour. It is important to try to understand this together as parents, not as people in conflict. For example:

– some children can find the transition from seeing one of their parents to being with the other very hard and show their distress. This distress is sometimes interpreted by one parent as a sign that a child does not want to see the other, whereas it more likely means that the child finds it hard leaving one for the other;
– the birth of a new baby can produce very mixed feelings for most children in a family as they wrestle with their concerns about whether they will still be special to their mother and father now that they are competing for their time with the newcomer. Children need to hear that they are loved by both of you;
– the introduction of a new adult, like a new baby, also brings a change in relationships, the time available for everyone may seem limited and anxieties can increase about still being loved, special and cared for;
– changes in financial and material circumstances can have an impact, both on the children and also between you as parents if there is a feeling that one of you is better off than the other;
– one parent moving home can raise a lot of fear and uncertainty about practical matters, such as how and when children can visit, particularly if one is moving abroad or a long distance away.

Making any plan stick is hard work and any of the above can create the need to review arrangements. Trying to negotiate and communicate about your children may not be easy especially soon after separation and especially if it was something you found difficult to do even when you were living together. Indeed, some of you may feel it would be better for you not to see and speak to each other at all, but . . . it will help the children if you do manage to communciate and reach an agreement. You will not, of course, force children to comply with it; they will surely rebel! They need support and encouragement from you both to try living in this 'new' way. Above all they need to know it is alright for them to love you both as parents and to like step-parents as friendly adults in their lives.

WILL YOU WRITE DOWN YOUR ARRANGEMENTS?

If you find it easy to communicate and can make simple arrangements that you agree about and which the children can remember, you may not need to write anything down. Your arrangements might look like this:-

If you can communicate easily but need to get quite complicated weeks sorted out your arrangements could look like this and could stick on the fridge door in both homes like this:

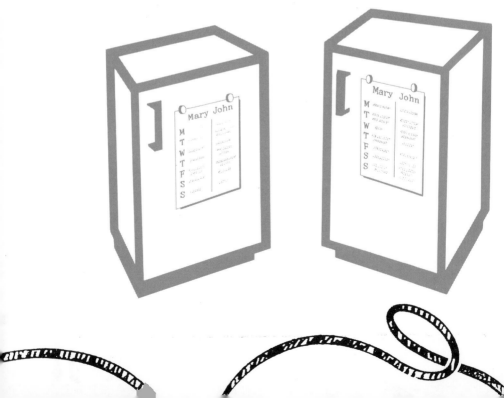

You might find communicating difficult and be in serious disagreement about arrangements. A Family Mediation Service will help you to reach a simple agreement which would be written down, with you, like this:-

Brockney Family Mediation
55 The High Street
Brockney
Tel 081 541 3601   June 2nd 1992

● Mark and Carolyn Baker's arrangements for John and Mary

We have agreed that John and Mary will spend most of their time during the week with Mark so that he can get them to and from school as long as he continues to live so near the school. Carolyn will have them with her every weekend and whenever Mark is away on business, as long as he gives her no less than one week's notice. If Mark moves, we will return to the Brockney Mediation Service to review these plans.

Some families want to set out a lot of things in detail and write all their decisions down so that they and their children feel they have some clear and long term parenting plans to rely on. They might use a Family Mediation Service to help them get it all written down, with the children looking at it in a family session, adding some of their ideas. It might be like this:-

● John and Mary's arrangements for Jo and Jemma

We, John and Mary Godden, in ending our marriage are resolved to work together to ensure that we help and support each other to care for our children, Jo and Jemma. We have therefore made the following plans for Jo and Jemma after our separation. We, as parents, recognise that things do change, that children can get upset, and sometimes may misbehave. When they get upset or if there are behavioural problems we take responsibility to discuss this together.

Homes – Mary will stay at 54 Beatrice Road with the children and John will live in a flat at 256 Hawk Road. We will continue to sort out the financial arrangements for this with our solicitors (or family mediator) and we intend that John will furnish his flat so that the children will also feel at home there.

Money – We will work out a fair way of sorting out the financial cost of looking after the children with our solicitors.

Everyday arrangements –
● Mary will see that Jo and Jemma get to and from school, but will ask John for help when she needs it.
● Jo and Jemma will stay with John at the flat every other weekend and John will take Jo to football every Saturday. On the weekends when Jo is with him, he will wash Jo's kit.
● Mary will take Jemma to the music club on Saturday mornings.
● John will take both children to the swimming club with him on Wednesdays as usual.
If there is ever a problem in doing this we will contact each other during the week in good time to make fresh plans.
● Pop and Nana Godden will invite Jo and Jemma for Sunday lunch at the weekends when they are with John, and Nana and Grandad Finch will visit them at Mary's as often as they do at present.

Holidays – We wish arrangements for Christmas and Easter holidays to be flexible. We should like to have some special time each with the children on these occasions. This year, Mary will have them with her on Christmas Eve and Christmas Day and John will have them overnight on Christmas Day and on Boxing Day.

During the summer this year, Mary will take them to Wales with Nana and Grandad Finch for three weeks in August and John will take them to Eastbourne for the last week of July and have them with him at his home for the last week of August.

Pets – Moggy (the cat) will stay at Beatrice Road, although John will look after him, by arrangement, whenever Mary, Jo and Jemma go away on holiday.

New partners – If either of us intends to live with another partner, we undertake to inform the other and meet to discuss how we can together support our children in adjusting to this major change to our childrens' lives. We undertake that we will always view each other as the parent of our children and will seek to ensure that, in the event of other adults entering their lives, this precious relationship with each of us will be protected.

School – We wish to share all the information from school and will continue to make joint decisions about their schooling and any other decisions about their welfare. Mary will notify the school of this.

Medical and dental treatment – except in an emergency, we will make mutual decisions about any medical or dental treatment.

Changes – we agree to notify each other at least one week in advance of any changes in any arrangements we have made. If any dispute arises that we cannot resolve ourselves, we will return to the family mediation service to sort it out.

Signed: Dated:

HOW WILL YOU USE THE ARRANGEMENT?

The value of making such arrangements is that they are jointly negotiated by you as parents and that they are written down, you and your children can use them as a secure basis for the present and the future. They represent your joint plans as parents based on your view at the time of what is in the best interests of each of your children.

These sorts of arrangements are very different from the old court arrangements whereby one parent got 'custody' and the other got 'access'. They are based on the understanding that parenting is a continuing role for both of you and that the needs of your children will be best met by your working together.

If you think you cannot sort out arrangements smoothly because you and your ex-partner cannot communicate well enough as a result of your separation or divorce then please do seek help from one of the many services and groups of people who can help you and your children.

Arrangements that are written down can also be useful for your solicitors, if you have them, and for the Court and can result in no Court Order being needed. (See legal section, page 50).

SORTING OUT FINANCE AND PROPERTY

Money can be a real source of difficulty when you are separating. If you only have one income then it will have to stretch over two households. If there are two incomes you have to work out how to balance the total amount of money available with the total amount of expenditure involved. If you need help to reach agreement about financial and property matters then you should approach a family solicitor and/or a family mediator for "comprehensive mediation". You can find out what is available in your local area by contacting one of the organisations listed at the end of this book (the Family Mediators Association, the National Family Conciliation (Mediation) Council, or the Solicitors Family Law Association).

"Comprehensive mediation" is detailed about your financial matters. You will be asked to sign that you will disclose

all your financial details to one another and to the mediator and that you will get legal advice (if not already using a solicitor) on any proposals reached.

"Comprehensive mediation" begins by you drawing up a budget of what income you have coming in and what you have going out, or will have going out, after you have separated. It will include all the costs associated with the children. You will also work together to identify the value of your assets including your house. If, as is often the case, there is a gap between what you have and what you need, the mediators will help you negotiate about how you can close that gap.

You will also be invited carefully to consider how to divide your assets in such a way that the needs of your children and yourselves are fairly met. What you jointly propose to do as a result of mediation is set out in the form of a "Memorandum of Understanding". This is not a legally binding document unless and until you obtain legal advice upon it.

The new Child Support Act, which requires parents to take financial responsbility for all their children, has introduced a formula for calculating how much child maintenance should be paid by each parent. It is a very complicated formula to be introduced in April 1993 through a Child Support Agency which will also chase up outstanding maintenance on behalf of the parent looking after the children. If you want to know more you need to consult a family solicitor or wait for the Child Support Agency to be set up and become active.

WHO CAN HELP YOU AND WHO NEEDS TO KNOW?

Every family deals with unhappiness, loss and change in its own way. Some of you have probably tried to protect your children from knowing that you and your ex-partner were unhappy and so your separation might have come as a sudden and unexpected shock to them. Some of you may have been locked in a partnership over many years where there has been verbal or physical violence. Your children may have been caught up in some of those battles between you. Some of you may have experienced the separation of your own parents or already been separated before and the pain from this separation may bring back memories of previous unhappy relationships and events.

None of us want to intrude in other people's lives and you may not want people outside your immediate family getting involved in a personal matter which you want to keep private. However, we certainly know within STEPFAMILY that struggling to cope alone can be lonely, frightening and very dispiriting. There are now many family and parent organisations that you can turn to either anonymously through their helplines, at a distance as a member receiving newsletters or buying leaflets and books, or in person by attending a training workshop or going to a local support group.

Each of your children will no doubt react differently to your separation. All the people who know your children and who have care of them will also want to help if they see your child in distress. They may need to ask you about what is happening in order to find appropriate ways of helping your child and some parents find it helpful to seek advice on how to handle their child's questions.

Teachers, doctors, health visitors, school nurses, playgroup leaders, day care staff, all know the importance of confidentiality. They also need to balance your need for privacy and the needs of your children for support and reassurance at times of acute stress. Most workplace nurseries, nursery schools, day care centres or childminders have a welcoming procedure explaining how everything is organised in the best interest of the children and they usually ask you to keep them informed of any major changes at home. With young children this is particularly important so that they can provide extra time and reassurance as well as keep a familiar routine and continuity for your child. Many children do become a little wistful, or tearful or naughty while they are trying to adjust to the changes at home.

We have already mentioned several times in this book that you might want to get help and support from friends, family or others. We have listed a wide range of organisations at the back of this book who provide help and information which may be of use to you at this time.

We also suggested that there were other people to think about when drawing up your parenting arrangement. John and Mary wanted to continue joint links with the school and Mary agreed to inform the school of this. As each of you continues to have parental responsibility even though you are living apart it is sensible to let everyone who may have care of your children at any time know where you can both be contacted in times of emergency or when parental consent is needed for whatever event.

The list may seem long because you will have built it up over a long period of time and, of course, you will add to it as the children grow into new activities and have new needs.

All that is needed is a simple statement to the effect that you and your ex-partner have separated but will be sharing all parental responsbility for your children. You can be contacted at one address and your ex-partner at another (details of which you will obviously enclose).

You can then ask for any specific requirements and offer to provide stamped addressed envelopes if mailing both of you appears to be a problem.

For example:

School – you can ask the school to inform you solely of any health checks, details of school trips, requests for financial contributions for trips or outings. Confirm how you wish to be addressed. Many children find it upsetting when school letters are given to them to take home still addressed to both parents.

You can also ask them to send two sets of invitations to parent meetings, sports day, presentation awards, open days etc, to each of you at your separate addresses. If you or your ex-partner already have a new partner you may wish to ask for two tickets each in order that your children can also share these events with their step-parents.

Teachers are responsible for children whilst they are at school and they need to know if different people may be collecting and delivering them. If there is a change in arrangements it is helpful to let the school know. It can also help your children if their teacher is aware that they are spending weekends with their other parent as it may account for their withdrawn or disruptive behaviour on a Friday or a Monday as they adjust to the comings and goings.

Health – your GP, the health visitor for younger children, and the school nurse can also be a useful source of advice and support both to you and your children. They are all concerned for the general well-being of your child as well as their physical health. Just as adults may benefit from self-help groups and talking with others in the same boat, it sometimes helps children to know they are not alone. A school nurse can often find ways of creating a small group where discussions around family life and relationships can lead to an informal sharing of experiences which may reduce stress and allow fears to be raised and addressed.

Activity, youth and community groups – if your children attend out of school activities the people in charge will also need to know who to contact at times of emergency or for parental consent. As we saw in John and Mary's parenting agreement it is quite likely that one parent will take responsbility for different activities for each of the children. The people who have responsbility for your children whilst they are in their care need to know who to contact first in any emergency and how to get hold of you both if necessary.

Family Mediation – to sort out issues concerning separation and arrangements for the children, and

Comprehensive Mediation – to sort out financial and property matters at the same time, are both available in many places. Your local CAB (Citizen's Advice Bureau) or solicitor or the organisations already mentioned and listed at the end of this book will have information about these.

Courts – If you and your partner are unable to reach any satisfactory agreements together about your children, mediation has been unable to help and it is necessary for one of you to go to Court it will clearly be important to let all the above people know precisely what the situation is with regards to your children. This may be particularly true if you have obtained a specific issues or prohibited steps order. However, if you have a contact order it may be possible for some of the above people to help you arrange contact with your children if this is still proving to be a problem.

Reading this through it must begin to seem to you that everything you do as a parent is being observed by others, and your relationship with your children is being organised so that it is no longer spontaneous. That should not be the case, but trying to help children move between two homes on a regular basis and keep up contact with both parents can take some organising.

The main reason for a parenting arrangement is to enable those delicate parenting threads to be kept intact, to be protected and supported. The purpose is to ensure a firm basis for the children so that they feel secure. A written parenting arrangement can also provide a safety net for you all if things get difficult. Turning to others for advice or help, keeping people informed about what is going on are ways of trying to support everyone at a time of change which is nearly always stressful.

Indeed, far from curbing spontaneity most parents soon develop new interests and friends and many form new relationships far quicker than they might have imagined. A great many parents will have developed a new relationship within two or three years of their separation and the impact of that process on your children is the focus of the next chapter.

NEW PARTNERS AND STEPFAMILIES

The end of a relationship is almost always accompanied by a period of sadness and feelings of failure. When a partner dies there is usually a funeral, which acknowledges the relationship and allows a sharing of grief. For the person who separates (or divorces) there is rarely a ritual from which to gain comfort. For those who divorce, there is the declaration of the granting of a divorce during the legal process – but that is all.

TAKING TIME

Some people already have a new partner in mind at the time their previous relationship ends, and perhaps this was the reason for it ending. When this is the case, everyone, adults and children, will have many adjustments to make all at the same time. Taking time also allows new partners, who may become step-parents, to meet the children, and for the newly separated family to prepare children for the arrival of a new partner for their father or mother. In other situations you may meet someone new later, after a period of being single again. In order to pick up the threads of parenting it helps for parents and children to have time together in the new situation of single parent households – both full and part time.

Following a separation or divorce, many have to give up the family home and move to smaller single parent households, a move which may be both sad and disruptive for everyone in the family. Some parents remain with their children in the family home, at least for a time, while the other, at least for a period, may have no home which their children can visit. It is difficult to be a parent only in a public place.

For some parents, usually those for whom the ending of the marriage has been an unwanted and devastating blow to self esteem, it can be difficult to pluck up courage to meet new people, let alone contemplate starting a new relationship. A new partnership raises all the old pains and fears arising from the failure of the previous relationship.

In any partnership, moving in together is a risk. There inevitably will be fears that it won't work this time either. This is especially worrying for parents whose children live with them as there are possible difficulties for the children to consider. Even when you meet someone new and are ready to make a new partnership, the children may not have come to terms with the divorce or the death sufficiently to treat the newcomer with

open mindedness. Indeed, for some children, this is the final blow to hopes that their parents might get back together again, and in their anger and sadness they make it difficult for someone they see as an intruder.

PREPARING THE CHILDREN

Little is known about what it is like for children when a parent's friend becomes lover and then step-parent. Even if children have become used to having separate relationships with their parents they may find it difficult to include a newcomer unless this is very carefully handled. It helps to be aware of the age and stage of development of the children as well as the state of the relationship between the two parents. Introducing a new partner may mean changing arrangements made at the time of the separation or divorce and this needs sensitive handling. Even then it can be difficult.

It can be even more difficult when events overtake the best laid plans.

Mandy and Michael have two daughters aged four and two. When Michael was promoted to a new post it meant he lived away from home during the week, coming home at the weekends and for holidays. The girls became used to him being away from home. When he began an affair with a much younger woman and the marriage broke down, they were already used to his absence and were relatively unaffected.

Mandy decided to petition for a divorce, and both parents explained to the girls what was about to happen; the girls quite happily went to stay with Michael every other weekend.

It was agreed by the parents that the children should not meet Michael's lover, Janey, until the divorce was final and Mandy and the children had moved from the family home into a new home, some distance from where they had all lived together.

However, on a weekend visit, Janey, perhaps jealous of Michael's close attachment to his daughters, came to his house very late one evening. Katie, the four year old, woke in the night and went to her father to be comforted, she found Janey there. When she returned to her mother's home she told her that Janey was Daddy's old friend, not the new friend Mummy and Daddy had said might come along one day. Katie also reported that Janey did not sleep in Daddy's whole bed, only part of it! Mandy rang Michael angrily to protest that he had broken their agreement. Michael explained what had happened. After some discussion, Mandy was able to accept the new relationship openly with her daughters.

Kate Rowan tells of young love revisited

Meeting the folks

First Person

The Doorbell rings, releasing a flood of long-buried memories. I am transported back 25 years to a similar state of nervous apprehension, waiting for my teenage boyfriend to be subjected to the scrutiny of critical parents. Only now it is not my parents who sit in judgment but my teenage children.

"It's him!" they cry, unnecessarily. In an agony of trepidation, I head for the door, acutely aware that, like my parents all those years ago, my children have infinite power to embarrass and show me up.

The slant of the earlier interrogation had been different. Respectability, steadiness, career prospects did not come into it this time. "Is he trendy?" the children asked. "Does he like rap?" "I bet he's bald!"

"Does he fancy you?" Their faces are incredulous. Love is for the young; at 40 it's a joke: "A boyfriend! You're too old."

How do you describe him? "Friend" is too coy and ambiguous, "partner" somewhat premature. I can't quite bring myself to call him "my fella". Perhaps the old-fashioned "suitor" should be brought back into use, or some modern equivalent invented.

I brace myself and open the door. Introductions are superfluous but I make them anyway, then hover uncertainly as silent appraisals are made. It is so important that they should like each other and first impressions can be hard to shake.

Will they fear he is taking me away from them, as perhaps my parents did? Will he be deterred if their behaviour is less than perfect? I am aware of the need to appear a good mother as well as an attractive woman. Do the children realise the power they wield?

After a few minutes they scuttle upstairs — to compare notes, no doubt. Is it safe to risk a hug now? We settle on the sofa but it is difficult to relax. We pull apart guiltily at the imagined creak of a footstep on the stairs. How well I remember the need for quick reactions, ears constantly pricked for the sound of snooping parents. The children are my moral guardians now.

Later, I anxiously seek their verdict. "He's OK, but he's not really your type," I am told. I wasn't aware I had a "type" but if it means he's different from their father, I won't argue. I dare not ask him what he thinks, but, "They're nice kids" he volunteers. What on earth was I worrying about?

The first hurdles are over, but more problematic questions loom ahead. At what stage should I openly share my bed? Will it induce shock, trauma, icy disapproval? Or will it be interpreted as licence for similar behaviour by them? The onus of parental responsibility is on me, I remind myself sternly. I am in a minefield my own parents and others of their generation rarely had to cross.

In the morning, my son has some astute and reassuring advice. "It'll do you good to have a boyfriend, Mum," he says sagely. "You'll be able to have some fun." I'm sure my parents never looked at it that way.

'Meeting the folks', Kate Rowan, was first published in the Guardian, 8th January 1992

BECOMING A STEPFAMILY

When parents marry or live with a new partner a stepfamily begins. A stepfamily is like a complex pattern - the more you look at it the more you see. You can think of a stepfamily as a combination of several families, like many patterns put together, making something new which has parts of other patterns.

Stepfamily members don't have to live under the same roof. Some stepfamilies consist of a parent and a new partner until children come to visit for weekends or holidays or even for a few hours. Others are made up of 'his' children, or 'her' children, and 'their' children as well, or all three – 'his', 'hers', and 'theirs'. The size and shape of a stepfamily can vary, even from day to day!

When a stepfamily begins, the adults have a new life together which they are happy about. The children may not feel the same way. Unless they are very young, the chances are that they will feel angry and sad and frightened: angry that a new person seems to have come into the place a father or mother was in, sad because the mother or father they have been with since their parents separated is preoccupied with a new partner and because they feel the loss of the parent not living with them, and frightened because they do not know what to expect or how they will fit into the new family.

Becoming a member of a stepfamily might be the biggest adjustment of all the changes we have described in this book. As we have seen, when changes are explained, children cope better. It is hard, though, for adults to find the right words. When

a parent is marrying or setting up house with a new partner, the words might be something like this:

'We are going to live together, but that doesn't mean I will stop being your Dad/Mum, or that we will not do things on our own sometimes. It will take a while for all of us to get used to but we can do it.'

WHO ELSE IS INVOLVED?

Sometimes others are angry and sad about the new stepfamily. Grandparents may be critical of the new family and afraid of losing contact with their grandchildren. Other family members may also react. Most concerned of all is the parent who no longer lives with the children. They are very likely to feel resentment about their children living with another adult, even if they were the one who chose to leave home or did not want the original separation to happen. The important thing to remember is that the sadness and anger becomes less as time goes on, especially if the children can spend time with both their parents and the parents can treat each other with respect.

Many parents who do not live with their children give up trying to maintain contact with them once a stepfamily comes into existence, or even before. They lose the thread of their parenting, although it is unlikely that either they or their children ever forget who they are to one another. Such parents do not stop being parents, but they stop doing it, perhaps in the mistaken belief that they are unnecessary to the children. Providing financial maintenance is one way of showing love and care for a child, but not the only one. It is continuing and reliable attention which matters most to a child. A little boy, whose father cancelled or altered arrangements for seeing him and his brother after a stepfamily was formed, asked his mother, "Does it mean that Daddy doesn't care about us anymore?"

It did not mean that, but children get hold of the wrong end of the stick. There are great difficulties in sharing children and in accepting that former partners have a new life with someone else. But **it is the children who lose when a parent cuts off although, and this may sound strange, everyone can gain when they do not!** When the adults understand that children need them all, and find ways to have satisfying contact, tensions are likely to disappear.

When children know that both parents will continue to care about them and look after them, their anger and suspicions begin to fade. Of course, there are circumstances when an

absent parent cannot be involved in decisions about his or her children, but usually, telephone calls and letters are possible, and this contact with them will help and is very important.

TIME FOR PARENTS AND CHILDREN

If you are creating a stepfamily you may want to make "one big happy family" from the two families coming together. This is understandable, but it seldom works. Children resent having to share their parent with a new partner, and possibly with step – brothers and sisters as well. All children like some time with their parents which is special to them, and it makes sense for step-parents to help this happen, even though it might be hard for them. Christine, for instance:

> Christine found it hard to share her partner, Garry, on the weekends when his thirteen year old son, Darren, came to stay with them. Garry and Darren made models together, littered up the dining room, but Darren hardly spoke to her. There was a feeling of tension but Darren obviously wanted his father's company.
>
> Christine found ways to occupy herself so that father and son could be alone together, but when she began an Open University degree she used the dining room for study. Conflict! Christine decided to study in the bedroom on condition that they left the dining room tidy after their modelling activities. It worked, and no one had to be discounted.

New rules about privacy and respect for individual preferences need to be worked out to safeguard activities, interests, and territory, with an appropriate sense of place and history. This applies to adult "children" as well as the young ones.

> Jennifer's grown-up children hardly went home when she remarried and Tom became their stepfather. Their home was exceedingly important to them both, but especially to Tom, whose childhood was marked by many moves. He felt their home was the first 'real' one he had ever had. When any of Jennifer's children came he made comments about their untidiness, complained about their table manners, and interrupted conversations with their mother, particularly when they were talking about old times.
>
> All the young adults were building separate lives from their parents, something which Jennifer found hard to accept because of her guilty feelings about leaving them with their father when her marriage ended. The three young people in turn were resentful about being criticised and they felt they were being told what to do by someone with no authority or right. Although they were pleased for their mother in her newfound happiness, they did not want to take part in it except for family festivals.

FEAR OF LOSING ONE'S CHILDREN

Parents often fear losing their children to a step-parent. Separation or divorce tends to undermine self confidence, and a step-parent who tries to become a replacement parent provokes fears that the children are being encouraged to change their loyalties and perhaps their residence, leaving one parent for another. Unless the children are very young and have no contact with their other parent it rarely happens that a step-parent takes a parent's place in the children's minds and hearts.

If you are an incoming step-parent, you therefore need to make your own individual relationship with each of your partner's children, and one which does not take over or compete with either of their parents. This takes time and care.

LIFE CAN BE JUST ONE PROBLEM AFTER ANOTHER

Inside a stepfamily things often go well at first. Then a crisis arises, usually about a child's behaviour, which reveals confusions about who is in charge and who will make decisions. Step-parent and stepchildren need time to become familiar with and used to one another. Step-parents are in no position to discipline until that happens.

Parents who have managed on their own know a great deal about looking after their children, and they need to retain this knowledge in a newly formed stepfamily. What they know is good, and their strengths will be the wisdom they need in the stepfamily. The adults can work together in planning and sharing responsibilities in the household, and it is necessary and comforting to do so, but they do not share the parenting of the children as if both had always been there.

STEPFAMILIES ARE DIFFERENT

They must find their own ways of working things out. This takes time, and time makes it easier, for both children and adults. It is not adding people to children's lives, but taking important people away, that is hard for them to accept. Children who are old enough to remember a parent, and as earlier sections of this book show, such memories are laid down at an early age, need their step-parent to care for them in such a way as not to challenge their feelings and loyalties. And if they have contact with their other parent they need everyone to accept the fact and to allow them to talk about and share their experiences.

BECOMING A STEPFAMILY MEANS –

- **making a life together which is new but does not ignore or 'bury' the past.** It means getting to know one another and talking about 'how things used to be'. If you are the step-parent, you may feel left out at times, but a stepmother or stepfather can talk about their past life as well. Children love to hear adults reminisce about their own childhood.
- **gradually building rules and traditions which will be different from the original family or families.** There will be other rules, other traditions, for them to adhere to and learn when children have contact with other parents and households. This sounds impossibly complicated, but experience shows that if adults can cope with the differences then children can.
- **trying to refrain from criticising ex-partners when the children are within hearing.** The person being criticised is someone the children love.
- **being sure that the new partners have time to be together without children** some of the time. This is very important; otherwise the new relationship can be ignored in responding to the children. Adults need attention too.
- **remembering not to blame each other when things go badly**, but trying to understand if someone may feel left out, mixed up, or unimportant.
- **being aware that sexual matters are different in a stepfamily** because the new partners have a new and intense sexual relationship. Sometimes stepchildren can be sexually attracted to a step-parent, which the adults must handle very carefully so that the child does not feel blamed. Sometimes a step-parent may have sexual urges toward a stepchild. These must never be acted on. If they show it can be confusing and potentially harmful to the child and to the whole family. Outside help is then needed.
- **being ready to cope with yet more change.** Whether full or part-time, stepfamilies may need to renegotiate arrangements for sharing children.

Stepfamilies can sound like nothing but trouble. In story books they look pretty awful. On the other hand, there can be the wish or dream that stepfamilies will solve all problems. It is well to remember that there always have been stepfamilies and always will – children and adults need them. And many people who live in them, or grew up in them, know that a richness of family life is as possible in a stepfamily as in any other. It is a complicated pattern, full of surprising possibilities.

THE LEGAL ASPECTS
THE CHILDREN ACT 1989

The law about children is now governed by the Children Act 1989, which came into force on 14th October 1991. In cases where there are old divorce proceedings which were dealt with before 14th October 1991 and new issues arise these will now be dealt with under the rules of the Children Act.

The Children Act has changed the terms that are used legally to describe the legal relationship of children and adults, and the approach that the Court will adopt. The old terms "custody", "care and control" and "access" have gone. New terms are now used. These new terms are "parental responsibility", "residence order", and "contact order". The concepts which they cover are similar to the old terms but it is a mistake to think that they are exact replacements, just using new names.

One of the fundamental principles of the Children Act is that the Court should not interfere and make orders unless it seems better for there to be an order rather than no order at all. If parents can reach their own agreements about their children's living arrangements and when they should see the parent they do not live with, the Court is not going to make an order. It is only if you can't agree and it looks as though you will need an order to make sure that you both know where you stand that the Court will intervene and generally make an order. In all applications to the Court the first consideration is what is in the best interests of the child.

PARENTAL RESPONSIBILITY

"Parental responsibility" means exactly what it sounds like; it gives you all the parental rights and duties that exist in law, between a parent and a child. However it emphasises the practical responsibilities not the "rights".

A married couple who have children both automatically have "parental responsibility" for them, and this continues even after a divorce. This means that your role as parents should continue to be something that you share and consult each other about. The major decisions about the children should be made jointly.

A Court would be very reluctant to take away parental responsibility from either parent unless it was convinced that it was in the best interests of the child.

Where the parents of a child are not married only the mother automatically has "parental responsibility" but the father

can acquire it if the mother enters into an agreement to share it with him, or by a Court Order.

Other adults can also acquire parental responsibility by obtaining a Court Order. This is of particular importance to step-parents if they play an important role in their stepchildren's lives. Their responsibility can be recognised by the law, much more so than was possible before the Children Act. Parental responsibility can be shared by more than two people. (See page 12).

WHEN PARENTS CAN'T AGREE

If you cannot agree the arrangements for your children with your ex-partner the matter can still be referred to the Court, and the Judge can be asked to make a wide range of orders. Where possible you should have tried to resolve the issues between you with the help of mediator, before you resort to the court. In many Courts procedure also has a conciliation stage built into it in an effort to try to keep matters from going to fully contested hearings (unless they really have to).

COURT ORDERS

The Court can make any one or combination of the following orders. They are often referred to as Section 8 orders:

● A RESIDENCE ORDER

This says with whom the children will live and can last until each child reaches the age of 16.

● A CONTACT ORDER

This states that the children can have contact with the person named in the Order, and obliges the person with whom the children live to allow this. Contact can include letters and telephone calls as well as visits. If necessary the Court can lay down the times and dates and places for visits..

● SPECIFIC ISSUE OR PROHIBITED STEPS ORDER

The Court can limit the way parents or other people involved with children exercise their parental responsibility. For instance the issue of school or religious upbringing can be decided by the Court if parents cannot agree.

● A FAMILY ASSISTANCE ORDER

This is a short term Order for a Court Welfare Officer or a Social Services Department to advise and assist a family for about six months where they may need specialist help. It can only be made with the consent of the adults involved and is intended to help adults resolve those conflicts surrounding divorce or separation that will affect the children.

WHO CAN APPLY FOR AN ORDER?

A broad group of people is entitled to apply for Section 8 Orders, including:

- either parent, including an unmarried father
- any person with an existing Order for "custody or care and control"
- a married step-parent who has treated the child(ren) as though they were his or her own
- a person with whom the child(ren) have lived for a period of three years in total over the last five years PROVIDED the application is made within three months of the end of this period
- any person who has the consent of all the others with parental responsibility

Other people who do not come within these categories can still apply provided they get permission from the Court to make the application. Generally the Court will give leave if it looks as though it will be in the best interests of the child(ren).

WHAT THE LAW CAN'T DO

It is important to remember that the law has very limited powers. It cannot make people behave better toward each other. When decisions about children are before the Court it does not set out to "punish" or to "reward" parents for what has happened in the past. Instead the Judge will try to achieve a compromise which he or she thinks will be workable for the future. This generally means that neither parent gets what she or he wanted so you have to accept a middle ground which is imposed upon you.

The Children Act lays great emphasis on the function of conciliation because it is widely perceived by the Courts and lawyers, as well as their clients, that it generally will produce a more practical solution to the difficulties between parents.

By and large an agreement which you work out between you has a much better chance of being kept in the future than one which is imposed on both of you by a Court.

PARENTING AS A CONTINUOUS THREAD

If you have continued to read this far we hope you agree with us that parenting is like a thread that runs throughout our lives – from our childhood, through our children's childhood and into the future. It is not an easy job even when life is running reasonably smoothly. Caring for children and sharing the responsibility for them when you and your partner have separated and especially as you both start to develop new lives with new partners is very difficult.

Few of us go into a relationship expecting or wanting it to fail. Most people who have not been able to make a first marriage or parenting partnership work still believe in family life and many want to create a new family. Sadly, from our experience, the difficulty of doing this often without adequate emotional or financial support and without having really talked through and sorted out parenting arrangements after the separation brings a great deal of stress into the stepfamily and over half the remarriages end in another separation or divorce.

Being a parent is a very special and important role and responsibility. Being a child can be lonely and frightening if you do not know what is happening in your life and the important people – your parents – are so preoccupied with their own concerns they forget to keep you informed. We all want our children to have safe, happy and secure childhoods. We would all prefer that their childhoods were stable and had as little disruption as possible. But real life is full of change and disruption – parents move home, move jobs, people have accidents, get ill or die, best friends fall out with each other.

Children can and do learn to cope with growing up and facing some of the tragedies and traumas that life deals them. They can cope better with the support of their parents, family and friends. At the beginning of this book we mentioned three key words: information, communication and co-operation.

Our final message to you on behalf of yourself, your ex-partner, your new partner and your children is:

● *inform* those close to you about what you want, need and are going to do so that they are not left anxiously worrying and wondering

● *communicate* your plans, fears, hopes and anxieties in such a way that your ex-partner, new partner and children feel able to offer you support for your needs but can also feel able to express their needs, which may be in conflict with yours

● *co-operate* with each other as partners, as a family, as a team of people concerned about each other and who want the best possible arrangements for the children involved within the constraints or limited options available to you.

Good Luck!

BOOKS TO READ

More detailed lists of books available can be obtained from STEPFAMILY

BOOKS FOR CHILDREN

Most of these books are under £6.00 but some are more expensive. Check with your local bookshop or borrow it from the library.

JUNIOR BOOKS

Althea (1980) *I have Two Homes.* Dinosaur Publications, Cambridge.

Baum, Louis *Are we nearly there?* Bodley head .

Berman, Claire (1982) *What am I doing in a Stepfamily?* How two families can be better than one. Angus & Robertson.

Boyd, Lizi (1987) *The Not-So-Wicked Stepmother.* Picture Puffin, Penguin

Brown, Laurence Krasny & Brown, Marc (1986) *Dinosaurs Divorce, A Guide for Changing Families.* Collins.

Drescher, Joan. *My Mother's getting married.* Methuen.

Hogan, Paula. *Will Dad ever move back home?* Raintree.

Mahy, Margaret (1984) *"Stepmother" in Leaf Magic and Five Other Favourites,* Magnet.

Mark, Jan (1988) *The Twig Thing.* A Young Puffin, Read Alone, Penguin.

McAfee, Annalena & **Browne**, Antony. *The Visitors who came to stay,* Hamish Hamilton.

Newman, Marjorie (1987) *Family Saturday.* Gazelle, Hamish Hamilton.

Osman, Trudy (1990) *Where has Daddy gone?* Heinneman

Seuling, Barbara (1985) *Stepfamilies: What kind of Family is this?* Golden Wonder, Western Publishing Company, New York.

Wignell, Edel (1987) *Marmalade, Jet and the Finnies.* Gazelle, Hamish Hamilton.

MIDDLE SCHOOL

Blume, Judy (1972) *It's not the end of the world,* Piper.

Bradley, Buff (1982) *Where do I belong?* A Kid's Guide to Stepfamilies. Addison-Wesley, Massachusetts, USA.

Byars, Betsy (1981) *The Cybil War,* Bodley Head. or Puffin.

Danziger, Paula (1982) *The Divorce Express.* Heinemann.

Danziger, Paula (1985) *It's an Aardvark-Eat-Turtle World.* Heinemann.

Duder, Tessa (1985) *Jellybean.* Puffin Book, Penguin.

Fine, Anne. *Goggle Eyes,* Puffin.

Gunsell, Angela (1989) *Let's Talk About DIVORCE.* Aladdin Books.

Gunsell, Angela (1990) *Let's Talk About STEPFAMILIES,* Aladdin Books.

Hodder, Elizabeth (1990) *Stepfamilies, Understanding Social Issues.* Aladdin Books, Gloucester Press.

MacLachlan, Patricia (1985) *Sarah, Plain and Tall.* Puffin Book, Penguin.

McKean, Thomas (1990) *The Peggy Plot.* Mammoth paperback.

Mitchell, Ann (1986) *When Parents Split Up,* Divorce explained to young people. Chambers Teenage Information Series.

Morpurgo, Michael (1989) *Mr Nobody's Eyes.* Heinemann

Nostinger, Christine. *Marrying off Mother.* Beaver Books.

Nystrom, Carolyn. *Mike's lonely summer,* Lion Care Series.

Townsend, Sue (1984) *The Growing Pains of Adrian Mole.* Metheun. (1982) *The Secret Diary of Adrian Mole, aged 13¾* Metheun.

Tugenhadt, Julia (1990) *What Teenagers can tell us about divorce and stepfamilies.* Bloomsbury.

BOOKS FOR PARENTS AND STEP-PARENTS

SELF-HELP

Some of these books may be out of print but your library can obtain them for you. Those written before the Children Act 1989 was implemented are out of date with regard to legal points. Please see the "General" list below which includes a book about the 1989 Act. If you are seeking specific legal information you should check with a family law solicitor.

Burgoyne, Jacqueline (1984) *Breaking even: Divorce, your children and you*, Penguin.

Burns, Cherie (1987) *Stepmotherhood*, Piatkus.

De'Ath, E (1988) *Step-parenting*, A Family Doctor Booklet, British Medical Association.

Hodder, E (1985) *The Step-parents' Handbook*, Sphere. (1988) *Stepfamilies Talking*. Optima.

Inglis, Ruth (1986) *The Good Step-parent Guide*, Grafton Books.

Maddox, Brenda (1975) *Step-parenting: How to live with other people's children*, Unwin.

Raphael, Kate (1986) *A Step-parent's Handbook*, Sheldon Press.

Vaughan, Diane (1986) *Uncoupling: How relationships come apart*, Vintage Books.

Visher, E and **Visher**, J (1982) *How to win as a stepfamily*, Dembner Books.

Whelan, T & **Kelly**, S (1986) *A hard act to follow: Step-parenting in Australia today*, Penguin Books.

GENERAL

Burgoyne, J. and **Clark**, D. (1984) *Making a go of it: a study of stepfamilies in Sheffield,* Routledge & Kegan Paul.

Dimmock, B. editor, (1992) *A Step in Both Directions?* The impact of the Children Act 1989 on stepfamilies, The National Stepfamily Association.

Smith, D. (1990) *Stepmothering*, Harvester-Wheatsheaf.

FICTION

Many works of fiction are about steprelationships or include them in the story. It is not possible to find them all, or even any except by chance or because the title has the word "step" in it. We are looking for fiction which feature stepfather figures and will add them as we are able.

Blackwood, Caroline (1984) *The Stepdaughter*, King Penguin.

Hutchinson, R. C. (1984) *The Stepmother*, Zenith.

Pilcher, Rosamunde (1990) *The Blue Bedroom*, Collection of short stories. Coronet Books, Hodder & Stoughton.

Thayer, Nancy (1980) *Stepping*, Sphere Books.

Yonge, Miss Charlotte M. (1989) *The Young Stepmother*, Macmillan & Co. (The 1861 edition was titled The young stepmother; or a Chronicle of mistakes) Both editions can be obtained from libraries. A Victorian novel, but it contains some eternal truths!

OTHER RESOURCES

VIDEOS

TIMS – "Parting Company"
Tavistock Institute of Marital Studies
Tavistock Centre
120 Belsize Lane, London,
NW3 5BA
Telephone: 071 435 7111

TAPES

Teenagers and Step-parents, Tapes for parents
Teenagers and Divorce, Tapes for parents
Trust for the Study of Adolescence
23 New Road,
Brighton BN1 1W2
Telephone: 0273 680281

PLACES TO GO FOR HELP·

FOR INFORMAL ADVICE AND SUPPORT

Childline
Freepost 1111, London N1 0BR
Telephone: 0800 1111

Exploring Parenthood
Latimer Education Centre
194 Freston Road
London, W10 6TT
Telephone: 081 960 1678

Families need Fathers
C/O 42 Drury Lane
London, WC2B 5RN
Telephone: 081 886 0970

Family Careline
National Childrens Home,
85 Highbury Park,
London N5 1VD
Telephone: 061 839 3939
Telephone: 071 226 2033

Gingerbread
35 Wellington Street,
London WC2E 7BN
Telephone: 071 240 0953

Grandparents Federation
78 Cooks Spinney
Harlow Essex, CM20 3BL
Telephone: 0279 437145

Home Start
2 Salisbury Road
Leicester LE1 7QR
Telephone: 0533 554988

MATCH (Mothers Apart from Their Children), c/o BM Problems,
London WC1N 3XX

National Council for One Parent Families,
255 Kentish Town Road,
London, NW5 2LX
Telephone: 071 267 1361

Parent Network
44/46 Caversham Road
London, NW5 2DS
Telephone: 071 85 8535

Parentline
Rayfa House, 57 Hart Road
Thundersley, Essex, SS7 3PD
Telephone: 0268 757077

Scottish Council for Single Parents
13 Gayfield Square,
Edinburgh EH1 3NX
Telephone: 031 556 3899

Soldiers, Sailors and Airmen's Association,
19 Queen Elizabeth Street,
London SE1 2LP
Telephone: 071 403 8783

Strathclyde Stepfamily Association,
21a Chapel Street,
Airdrie, Glasgow G65 8HF
Telephone: 0236 48217

STEPFAMILY
72 Willesden Lane, London NW6 7TA
Telephone: 071 372 0844
Helpline 081 372 0846

FOR COUNSELLING OR THERAPY

Asian Family Counselling Service,
74 The Avenue, London W13 8LB
Telephone: 081 997 5749

Catholic Marriage Advisory Council
Clitherow House
1 Blythe Mews, Blythe Road
London W14 0NW
Telephone: 071 371 1341

National Council For the Divorced & Separated
1/3 High Street, Little Shelford
Cambridge, CB2 5ES
Telephone: 0533 708880

Institute of Family Therapy
43 New Cavendish Street
London, W1 7RG
Telephone: 071 935 1651

Jewish Marriage Council
529b Finchley Road,
London NW3 3LG
Telephone: 071 794 5222

London Marriage Guidance,
76a New Cavendish Street,
London W1M 7LB
Telephone: 071 580 1087

NationalAssociation of Young People's Counselling & Advisory Services (NAYPCAS),
17-23 Albion Street, Leicester LE1 6GD
Telephone: 0533 558763

RELATE Marriage Guiance
Herbert Grey College
Little Church Street, Rugby CV21 3AP
Telephone: 07885 73241/565675

Westminster Pastoral Foundation,
23 Kensington Square,
London W8 5HN
Telephone: 071 937 6956

Womens Counselling and Resource Centre,
1st Floor, McIver House,
Cadogan Street, Glasgow G2
Telephone: 041 227 6006

Local child and family guidance centres can be found in the telephone directory or from your local library, CAB or social services department.

FOR CONCILIATION OR MEDIATION

Family Conciliation Scotland,
127 Rose Street South Lane,
Edinburgh EH2 4BB
Telephone: 031 220 1610

Family Mediators Association,
will give you local agencies.
The Old House, Rectory Gardens,
Henbury, Bristol BS10 7AQ
Telephone: 0272 5000140

National Family Conciliation
Council, *will give you local agencies.*
Shaftesbury Centre,
Percy Street, Swindon SN2 2AZ
Telephone: 0793 514055

Solicitors Family Law Association,
PO Box 302,
Keston, Kent BR2 6EZ

Try also your local Citizens Advice
Bureau and Court Welfare Service
listed in your local telephone
directory or from your library

FOR LEGAL ADVICE

Children's Legal Centre,
20 Compton Terrace,
London N1 2UN
Telephone: 071 359 9392

Solicitors Family Law Association
PO Box 302,
Keston,
Kent BR2 6EZ

FOR WELFARE ADVICE

Child Poverty Action Group,
Fourth Floor,
1-5 Bath Street,
London EC1V 9PY
Telephone: 071 253 3406

Citizens Advice Bureau –
see telephone directory

Family Rights Group,
The Print House,
18 Ashwin Street,
London E8 3DL
Telephone: 071 923 2628

Local Department of Social
Services –
see telephone directory

INDEX

STEPFAMILY was founded in 1983 by a group of stepchildren and step-parents. The main aim is to provide information, advice and support to all those living in stepfamilies and those who work with them. We also offer help and advice to other family members such as – grandparents, aunts and uncles.

Over two and a half million children and young people will grow up in stepfamilies during the 1990s. Many will already have seen their parents separate and divorce and may find another change and disruption from lone parent to stepfamily difficult. Some children may have lost their parent through death. Both kinds of event can be very upsetting for children and can cause problems at home and at school.

Most people need some help when starting a family and a stepfamily is no different. We believe that it is important that when a stepfamily turns to anyone for help they should receive sensitive understanding of the differences between birth parent and step-parent.

STEPFAMILY is a very small and new charity which depends on donations and grants for its work. Please help us by becoming a STEPFAMILY sponsor:

£15	provides three hours of a telephone counsellor's time
£60	could send Helpline information to 100 schools or GPs
£100	would print 5000 Helpline posters so people know they are not alone
£500	would prepare and support a new telephone counsellor for a year

If you want to support our work or to know more about our services please tear off the form below and send it to:

STEPFAMILY, 72 Willesden Lane, London NW6 7TA.

- -

Please send me details of STEPFAMILY membership

Please send me information about:

☐ your range of publications
☐ how to become a volunteer telephone counsellor
☐ how to be a local STEPFAMILY contact
☐ how to set up a local support group
☐ training events and conferences

I would like to make a donation to keep STEPFAMILY services going and I enclose a cheque/postal order payable to STEPFAMILY for £ _____

Name _____

Address _____

_____ Post code _____